Hal•Leonard

JAZZ PLAY-ALONG®

Book and CD for B♭, E♭, C and Bass Clef Instruments

JAZZ COVERS ROCK

volume 158

Arranged and Produced by Mark Taylor

T0081993

BOOK

CD

PAGE N

ISBN 978-1-4584-0383-4

Hal•Leonard CORPORATION

7777 W. Bluemound Rd. P.O. Box 13819 Milwaukee, WI 53213

Visit Hal Leonard Online at
www.halleonard.com

JAZZ COVERS ROCK

Volume 158

Arranged and Produced
by Mark Taylor

Featured Players:

Graham Breedlove–Trumpet
John Desalme–Tenor Sax
Tony Nalker–Piano
Regan Brough–Bass
Jim Roberts–Guitar
Todd Harrison–Drums

Recorded at Bias Studios, Springfield, Virginia
Bob Dawson, Engineer

HOW TO USE THE CD:

Each song has <u>two</u> tracks:

1) Split Track/Melody

Woodwind, Brass, Keyboard, and **Mallet Players** can use this track as a learning tool for melody style and inflection.

Bass Players can learn and perform with this track – remove the recorded bass track by turning down the volume on the LEFT channel.

Keyboard and **Guitar Players** can learn and perform with this track – remove the recorded piano part by turning down the volume on the RIGHT channel.

2) Full Stereo Track

Soloists or **Groups** can learn and perform with this accompaniment track with the RHYTHM SECTION only.

BLACK HOLE SUN

WORDS AND MUSIC BY
CHRIS CORNELL

CD
❶ : SPLIT TRACK/MELODY
❷ : FULL STEREO TRACK

C VERSION

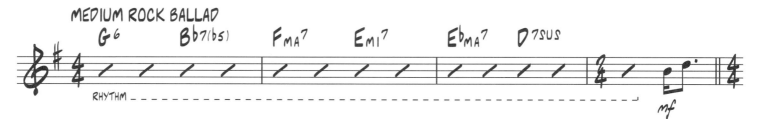

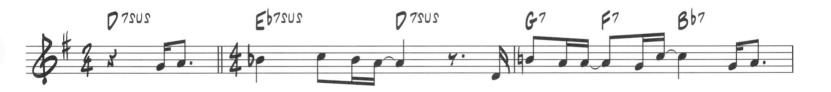

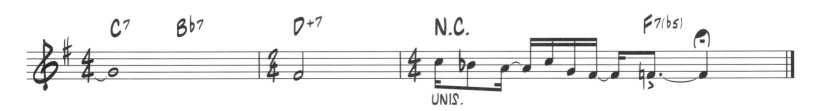

EVERY BREATH YOU TAKE

CD
⬦ 5 : SPLIT TRACK/MELODY
⬦ 6 : FULL STEREO TRACK

C VERSION

MUSIC AND LYRICS
BY STING

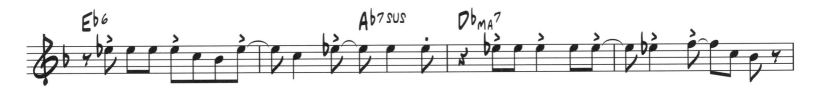

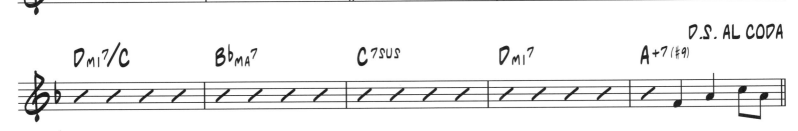

FLY LIKE AN EAGLE

WORDS AND MUSIC BY
STEVE MILLER

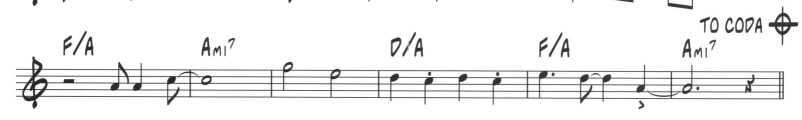
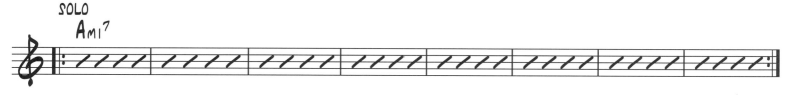

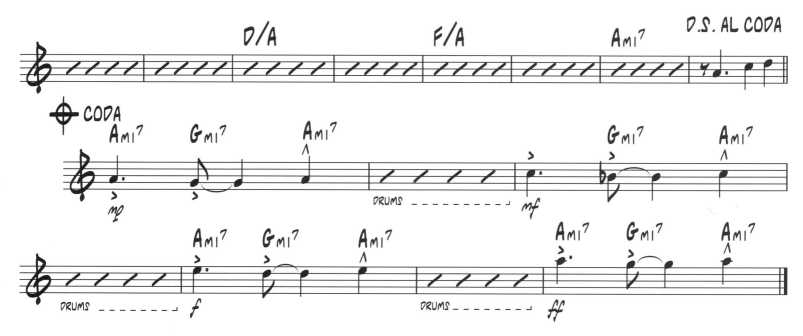

IT'S MY LIFE

WORDS AND MUSIC BY JON BON JOVI,
MARTIN SANDBERG AND RICHIE SAMBORA

Money

WORDS AND MUSIC BY
ROGER WATERS

C VERSION

DREAM ON

WORDS AND MUSIC BY
STEVEN TYLER

CD
◆ 3 : SPLIT TRACK/MELODY
◆ 4 : FULL STEREO TRACK

C VERSION

MEDIUM SALSA

RIT.

CD

: SPLIT TRACK/MELODY
: FULL STEREO TRACK

C VERSION

PINBALL WIZARD

WORDS AND MUSIC BY
PETER TOWNSHEND

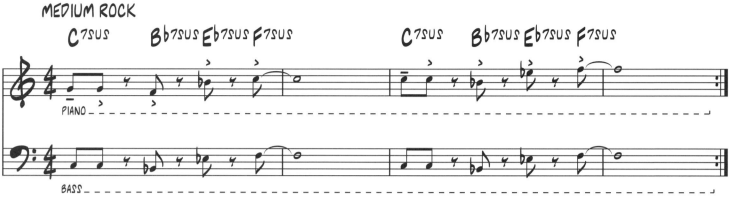

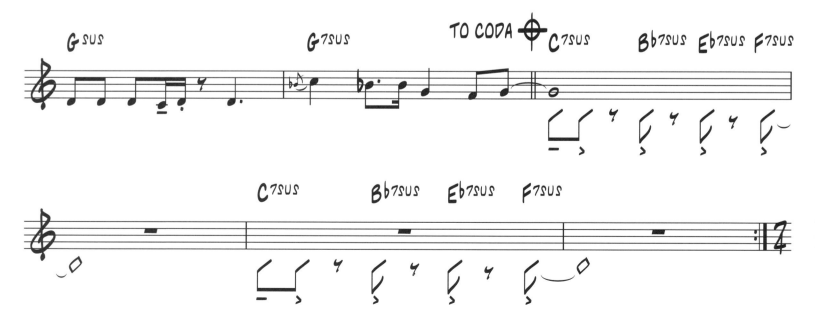

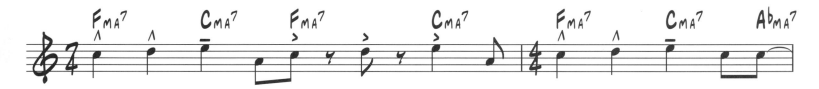

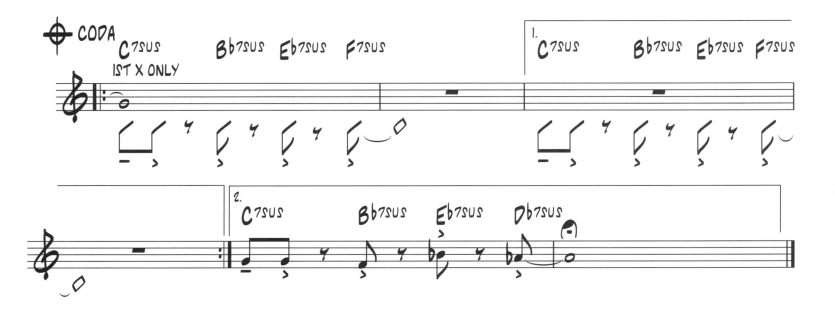

SMELLS LIKE TEEN SPIRIT

WORDS AND MUSIC BY KURT COBAIN,
KRIST NOVOSELIC AND DAVE GROHL

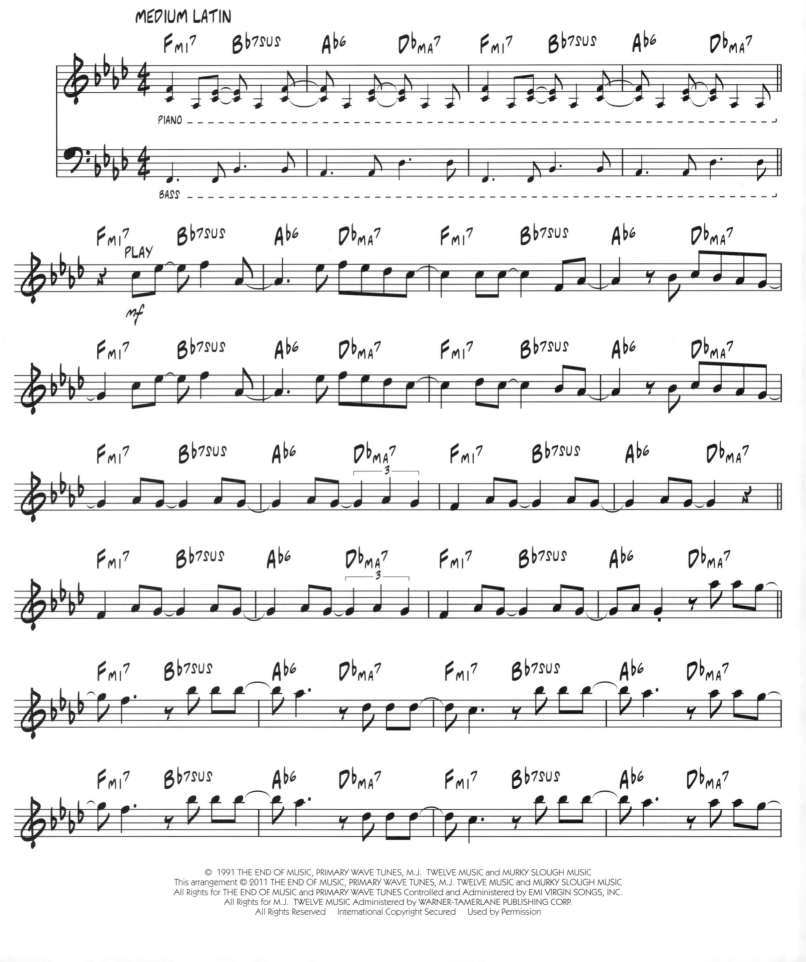

TO CODA ⊕

SOLOS (PLAY 6X'S)

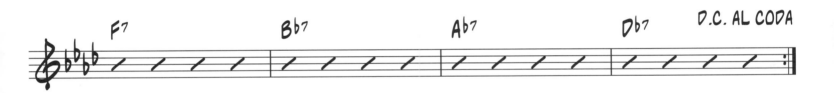

D.C. AL CODA

⊕ CODA

CD
⑰ : SPLIT TRACK/MELODY
⑱ : FULL STEREO TRACK

TAKIN' IT TO THE STREETS

WORDS AND MUSIC BY
MICHAEL McDONALD

C VERSION

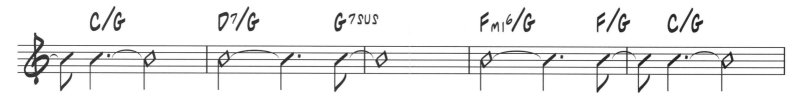

WONDERWALL

WORDS AND MUSIC BY
NOEL GALLAGHER

CD

19 : SPLIT TRACK/MELODY
20 : FULL STEREO TRACK

C VERSION

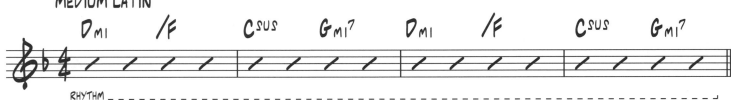

23

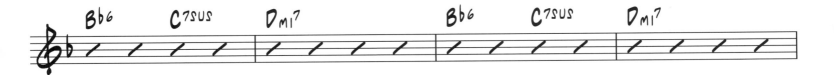

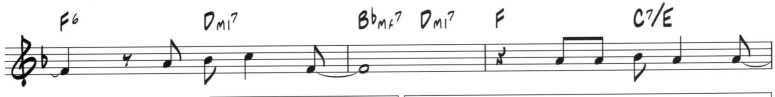

BLACK HOLE SUN

CD
① : SPLIT TRACK/MELODY
② : FULL STEREO TRACK

Bb VERSION

WORDS AND MUSIC BY
CHRIS CORNELL

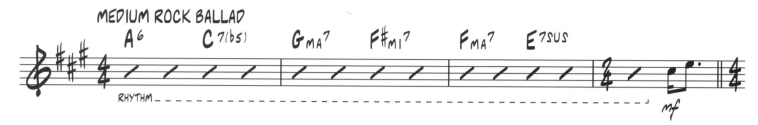

EVERY BREATH YOU TAKE

CD
- ◆5: SPLIT TRACK/MELODY
- ◆6: FULL STEREO TRACK

Bb VERSION

MUSIC AND LYRICS
BY STING

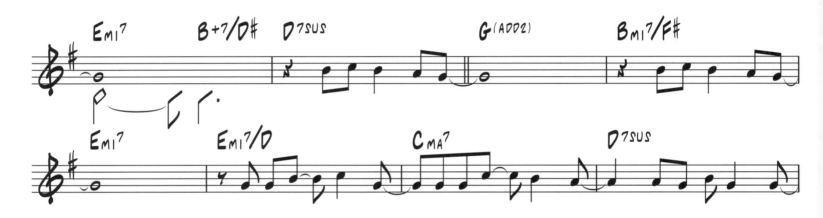

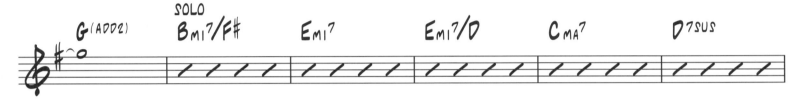

CD
7 : SPLIT TRACK/MELODY
8 : FULL STEREO TRACK

FLY LIKE AN EAGLE

WORDS AND MUSIC BY
STEVE MILLER

Bb VERSION

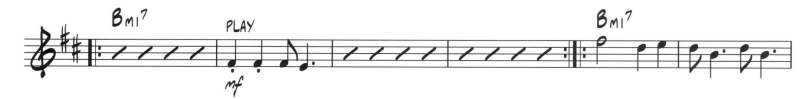

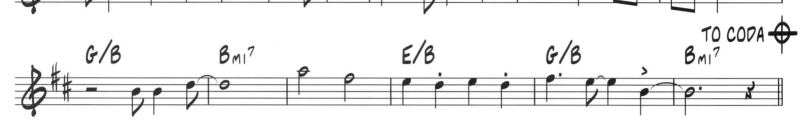

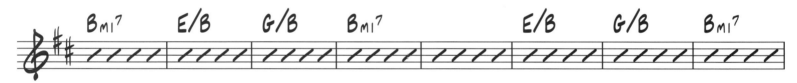

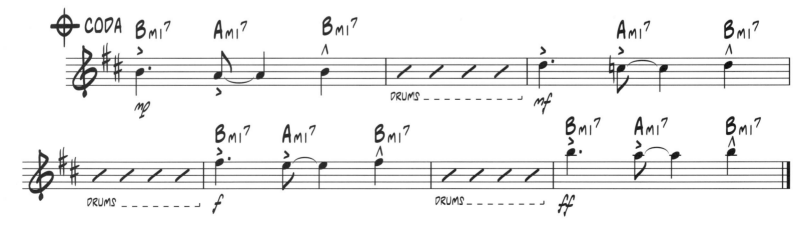

IT'S MY LIFE

WORDS AND MUSIC BY JON BON JOVI,
MARTIN SANDBERG AND RICHIE SAMBORA

Money

WORDS AND MUSIC BY
ROGER WATERS

CD
11 : SPLIT TRACK/MELODY
12 : FULL STEREO TRACK

Bb VERSION

CD
3: SPLIT TRACK/MELODY
4: FULL STEREO TRACK

DREAM ON

WORDS AND MUSIC BY
STEVEN TYLER

Bb VERSION

MEDIUM SALSA

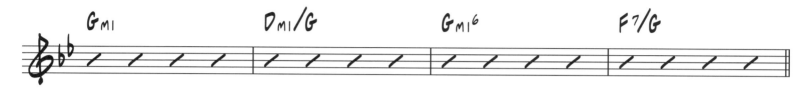

Pinball Wizard

WORDS AND MUSIC BY
PETER TOWNSHEND

Bb VERSION

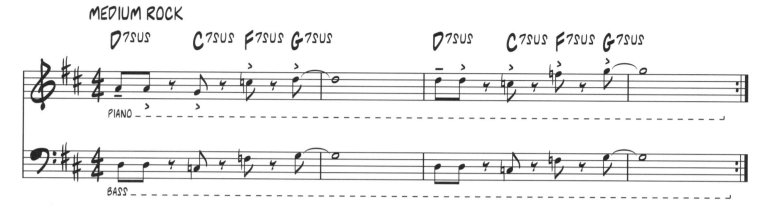

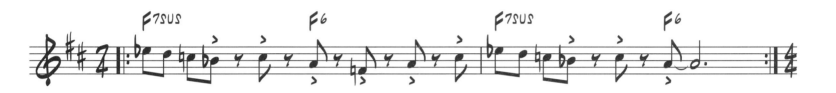

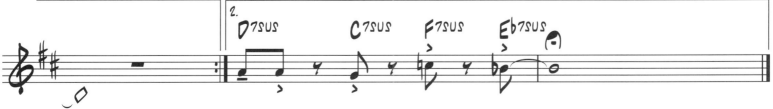

SMELLS LIKE TEEN SPIRIT

WORDS AND MUSIC BY KURT COBAIN,
KRIST NOVOSELIC AND DAVE GROHL

Bb VERSION

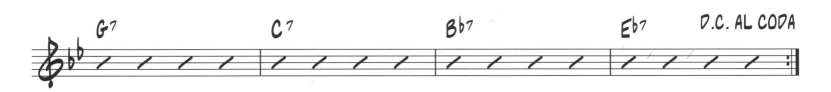

Takin' It to the Streets

CD
17 : SPLIT TRACK/MELODY
18 : FULL STEREO TRACK

WORDS AND MUSIC BY
MICHAEL McDONALD

Bb VERSION

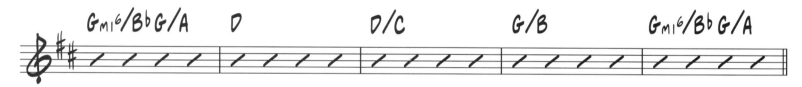

WONDERWALL

WORDS AND MUSIC BY
NOEL GALLAGHER

Bb VERSION

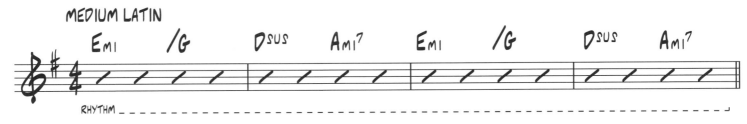

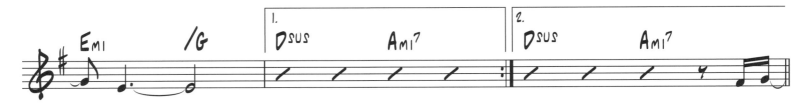

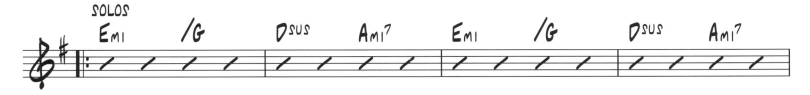

BLACK HOLE SUN

CD
1 : SPLIT TRACK/MELODY
2 : FULL STEREO TRACK

WORDS AND MUSIC BY
CHRIS CORNELL

Eb VERSION

MEDIUM ROCK BALLAD

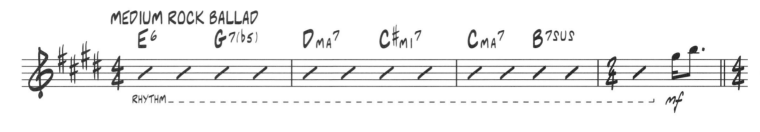

EVERY BREATH YOU TAKE

CD

5 : SPLIT TRACK/MELODY
6 : FULL STEREO TRACK

Eb VERSION

MUSIC AND LYRICS
BY STING

CD

7 : SPLIT TRACK/MELODY
8 : FULL STEREO TRACK

FLY LIKE AN EAGLE

WORDS AND MUSIC BY
STEVE MILLER

Eb VERSION

IT'S MY LIFE

WORDS AND MUSIC BY JON BON JOVI, MARTIN SANDBERG AND RICHIE SAMBORA

Money

WORDS AND MUSIC BY
ROGER WATERS

Dream On

WORDS AND MUSIC BY
STEVEN TYLER

Eb VERSION

MEDIUM SALSA

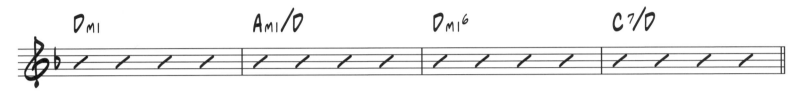

SOLOS (2 CHORUSES)

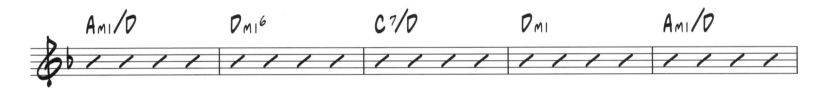

RIT.

CD

13: SPLIT TRACK/MELODY
14: FULL STEREO TRACK

PINBALL WIZARD

WORDS AND MUSIC BY
PETER TOWNSHEND

Eb VERSION

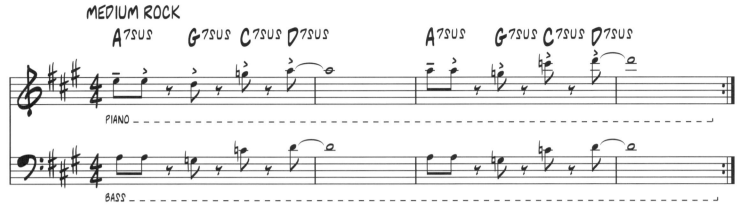

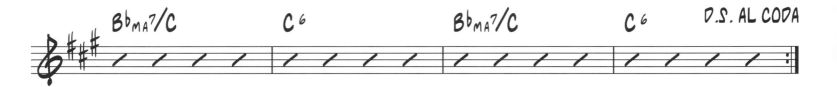

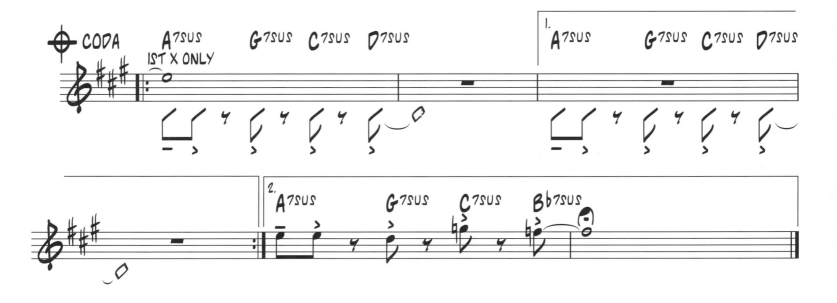

CD
15 : SPLIT TRACK/MELODY
16 : FULL STEREO TRACK

SMELLS LIKE TEEN SPIRIT

WORDS AND MUSIC BY KURT COBAIN,
KRIST NOVOSELIC AND DAVE GROHL

Eb VERSION

TO CODA

SOLO BREAK

SOLOS (PLAY 6X'S)

D.C. AL CODA

CODA

CD

Takin' It to the Streets

WORDS AND MUSIC BY
MICHAEL McDONALD

Eb VERSION

MEDIUM ROCK

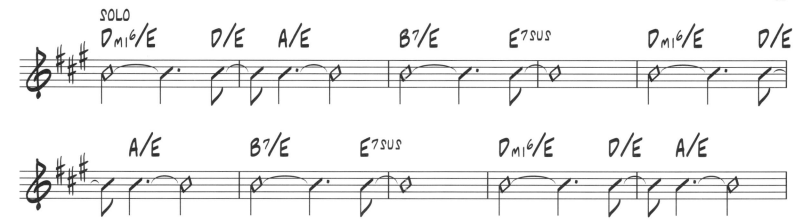

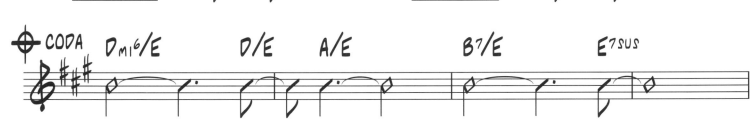

WONDERWALL

WORDS AND MUSIC BY
NOEL GALLAGHER

Eb VERSION

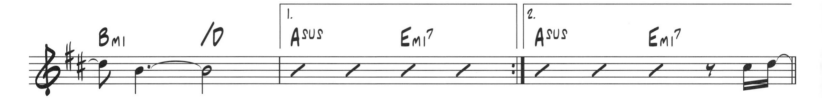

RIT.

Black Hole Sun

WORDS AND MUSIC BY
CHRIS CORNELL

65

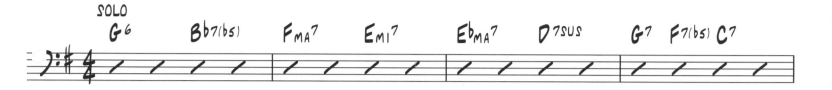

SOLO

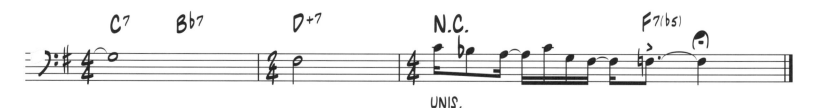

UNIS.

EVERY BREATH YOU TAKE

CD

⬧ 5 : SPLIT TRACK/MELODY
⬧ 6 : FULL STEREO TRACK

MUSIC AND LYRICS
BY STING

𝄢: C VERSION

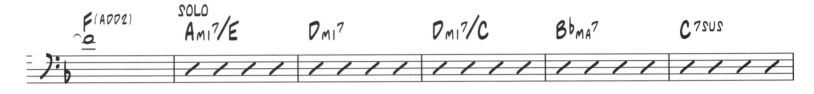

FLY LIKE AN EAGLE

WORDS AND MUSIC BY
STEVE MILLER

IT'S MY LIFE

WORDS AND MUSIC BY JON BON JOVI,
MARTIN SANDBERG AND RICHIE SAMBORA

Money

WORDS AND MUSIC BY
ROGER WATERS

Dream On

WORDS AND MUSIC BY
STEVEN TYLER

CD
3 : SPLIT TRACK/MELODY
◄ : FULL STEREO TRACK

𝄢 C VERSION

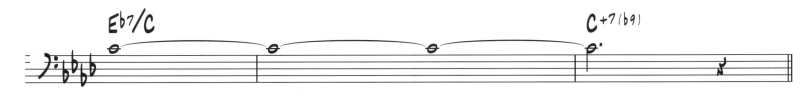

SOLOS (2 CHORUSES)

CD

🔷13 : SPLIT TRACK/MELODY
🔷14 : FULL STEREO TRACK

𝄢: C VERSION

PINBALL WIZARD

WORDS AND MUSIC BY
PETER TOWNSHEND

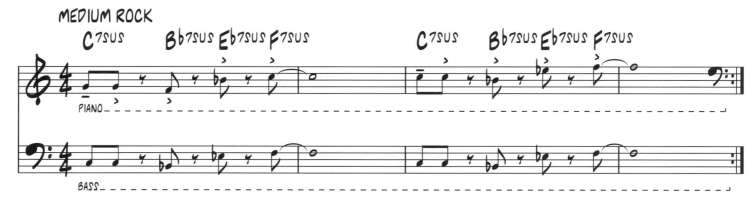

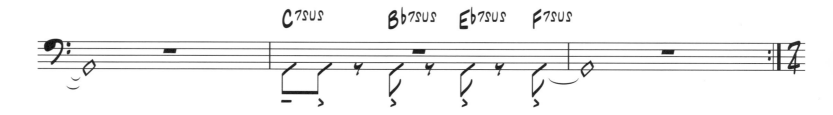

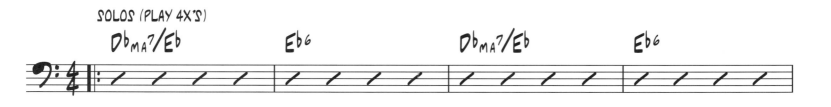

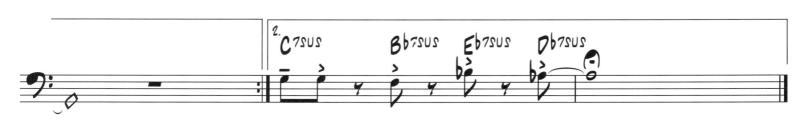

SMELLS LIKE TEEN SPIRIT

CD
- **15** : SPLIT TRACK/MELODY
- **16** : FULL STEREO TRACK

WORDS AND MUSIC BY KURT COBAIN,
KRIST NOVOSELIC AND DAVE GROHL

𝄢 C VERSION

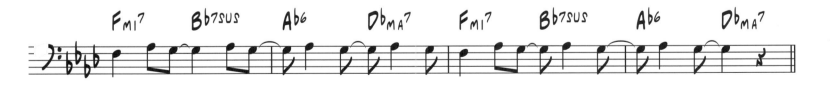

Takin' It To The Streets

WORDS AND MUSIC BY
MICHAEL McDONALD

SOLO

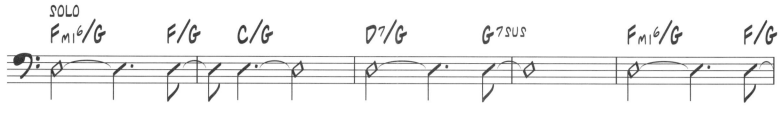

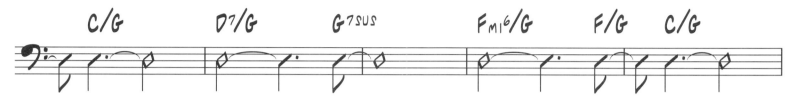

RIT.

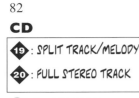

WONDERWALL

WORDS AND MUSIC BY
NOEL GALLAGHER

9: C VERSION

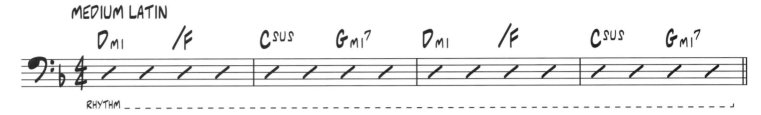

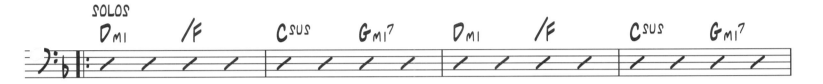

Presenting the Hal Leonard JAZZ PLAY-ALONG SERIES

For use with all B-flat, E-flat, Bass Clef and C instruments, the Jazz Play-Along® Series is the ultimate learning tool for all jazz musicians. With musician-friendly lead sheets, melody cues, and other split-track choices on the included CD, these first-of-a-kind packages help you master improvisation while playing some of the greatest tunes of all time. FOR STUDY, each tune includes a split track with: melody cue with proper style and inflection • professional rhythm tracks • choruses for soloing • removable bass part • removable piano part. FOR PERFORMANCE, each tune also has: an additional full stereo accompaniment track (no melody) • additional choruses for soloing.

1. DUKE ELLINGTON
00841644 .... $16.95

1A. MAIDEN VOYAGE/ALL BLUES
00843158 .... $15.99

2. MILES DAVIS
00841645 .... $16.95

3. THE BLUES
00841646 .... $16.99

4. JAZZ BALLADS
00841691 .... $16.99

5. BEST OF BEBOP
00841689 .... $16.95

6. JAZZ CLASSICS WITH EASY CHANGES
00841690 .... $16.99

7. ESSENTIAL JAZZ STANDARDS
00843000 .... $16.99

8. ANTONIO CARLOS JOBIM AND THE ART OF THE BOSSA NOVA
00843001 .... $16.95

9. DIZZY GILLESPIE
00843002 .... $16.99

10. DISNEY CLASSICS
00843003 .... $16.99

11. RODGERS AND HART FAVORITES
00843004 .... $16.99

12. ESSENTIAL JAZZ CLASSICS
00843005 .... $16.99

13. JOHN COLTRANE
00843006 .... $16.95

14. IRVING BERLIN
00843007 .... $15.99

15. RODGERS & HAMMERSTEIN
00843008 .... $15.99

16. COLE PORTER
00843009 .... $15.95

17. COUNT BASIE
00843010 .... $16.95

18. HAROLD ARLEN
00843011 .... $15.95

19. COOL JAZZ
00843012 .... $15.95

20. CHRISTMAS CAROLS
00843080 .... $14.95

21. RODGERS AND HART CLASSICS
00843014 .... $14.95

22. WAYNE SHORTER
00843015 .... $16.95

23. LATIN JAZZ
00843016 .... $16.95

24. EARLY JAZZ STANDARDS
00843017 .... $14.95

25. CHRISTMAS JAZZ
00843018 .... $16.95

26. CHARLIE PARKER
00843019 .... $16.95

27. GREAT JAZZ STANDARDS
00843020 .... $16.99

28. BIG BAND ERA
00843021 .... $15.99

29. LENNON AND MCCARTNEY
00843022 .... $16.95

30. BLUES' BEST
00843023 .... $15.99

31. JAZZ IN THREE
00843024 .... $15.99

32. BEST OF SWING
00843025 .... $15.99

33. SONNY ROLLINS
00843029 .... $15.95

34. ALL TIME STANDARDS
00843030 .... $15.99

35. BLUESY JAZZ
00843031 .... $16.99

36. HORACE SILVER
00843032 .... $16.99

37. BILL EVANS
00843033 .... $16.95

38. YULETIDE JAZZ
00843034 .... $16.95

39. "ALL THE THINGS YOU ARE" & MORE JEROME KERN SONGS
00843035 .... $15.99

40. BOSSA NOVA
00843036 .... $15.99

41. CLASSIC DUKE ELLINGTON
00843037 .... $16.99

42. GERRY MULLIGAN FAVORITES
00843038 .... $16.99

43. GERRY MULLIGAN CLASSICS
00843039 .... $16.95

44. OLIVER NELSON
00843040 .... $16.95

45. JAZZ AT THE MOVIES
00843041 .... $15.99

46. BROADWAY JAZZ STANDARDS
00843042 .... $15.99

47. CLASSIC JAZZ BALLADS
00843043 .... $15.99

48. BEBOP CLASSICS
00843044 .... $16.99

49. MILES DAVIS STANDARDS
00843045 .... $16.95

50. GREAT JAZZ CLASSICS
00843046 .... $15.99

51. UP-TEMPO JAZZ
00843047 .... $15.99

52. STEVIE WONDER
00843048 .... $16.99

53. RHYTHM CHANGES
00843049 .... $15.99

54. "MOONLIGHT IN VERMONT" AND OTHER GREAT STANDARDS
00843050 .... $15.99

55. BENNY GOLSON
00843052 .... $15.95

56. "GEORGIA ON MY MIND" & OTHER SONGS BY HOAGY CARMICHAEL
00843056 .... $15.99

57. VINCE GUARALDI
00843057 .... $16.99

58. MORE LENNON AND MCCARTNEY
00843059 .... $15.99

59. SOUL JAZZ
00843060 .... $15.99

60. DEXTER GORDON
00843061 .... $15.95

61. MONGO SANTAMARIA
00843062 .... $15.95

62. JAZZ-ROCK FUSION
00843063 .... $16.99

63. CLASSICAL JAZZ
00843064 ....$14.95

64. TV TUNES
00843065 ....$14.95

65. SMOOTH JAZZ
00843066 ....$16.99

66. A CHARLIE BROWN CHRISTMAS
00843067 ....$16.99

67. CHICK COREA
00843068 ....$15.95

68. CHARLES MINGUS
00843069 ....$16.95

69. CLASSIC JAZZ
00843071 ....$15.99

70. THE DOORS
00843072 ....$14.95

71. COLE PORTER CLASSICS
00843073 ....$14.95

72. CLASSIC JAZZ BALLADS
00843074 ....$15.99

73. JAZZ/BLUES
00843075 ....$14.95

74. BEST JAZZ CLASSICS
00843076 ....$15.99

75. PAUL DESMOND
00843077 ....$14.95

76. BROADWAY JAZZ BALLADS
00843078 ....$15.99

77. JAZZ ON BROADWAY
00843079 ....$15.99

78. STEELY DAN
00843070 ....$14.99

79. MILES DAVIS CLASSICS
00843081 ....$15.99

80. JIMI HENDRIX
00843083 ....$15.99

81. FRANK SINATRA – CLASSICS
00843084 ....$15.99

82. FRANK SINATRA – STANDARDS
00843085 ....$15.99

83. ANDREW LLOYD WEBBER
00843104 ....$14.95

84. BOSSA NOVA CLASSICS
00843105 ....$14.95

85. MOTOWN HITS
00843109 ....$14.95

86. BENNY GOODMAN
00843110 ....$14.95

87. DIXIELAND
00843111 ....$14.95

88. DUKE ELLINGTON FAVORITES
00843112 ....$14.95

89. IRVING BERLIN FAVORITES
00843113 ....$14.95

90. THELONIOUS MONK CLASSICS
00841262 ....$16.99

91. THELONIOUS MONK FAVORITES
00841263 ....$16.99

92. LEONARD BERNSTEIN
00450134 ....$15.99

93. DISNEY FAVORITES
00843142 ....$14.99

94. RAY
00843143 ....$14.99

95. JAZZ AT THE LOUNGE
00843144 ....V$14.99

96. LATIN JAZZ STANDARDS
00843145 ....$14.99

97. MAYBE I'M AMAZED*
00843148 ....$15.99

98. DAVE FRISHBERG
00843149 ....$15.99

99. SWINGING STANDARDS
00843150 ....$14.99

100. LOUIS ARMSTRONG
00740423 ....$15.99

101. BUD POWELL
00843152 ....$14.99

102. JAZZ POP
00843153 ....$14.99

103. ON GREEN DOLPHIN STREET & OTHER JAZZ CLASSICS
00843154 ....$14.99

104. ELTON JOHN
00843155 ....$14.99

105. SOULFUL JAZZ
00843151 ....$15.99

106. SLO' JAZZ
00843117 ....$14.99

107. MOTOWN CLASSICS
00843116 ....$14.99

108. JAZZ WALTZ
00843159 ....$15.99

109. OSCAR PETERSON
00843160 ....$16.99

110. JUST STANDARDS
00843161 ....$15.99

111. COOL CHRISTMAS
00843162 ....$15.99

112. PAQUITO D'RIVERA – LATIN JAZZ*
48020662 ....$16.99

113. PAQUITO D'RIVERA – BRAZILIAN JAZZ*
48020663 ....$19.99

114. MODERN JAZZ QUARTET FAVORITES
00843163 ....$15.99

115. THE SOUND OF MUSIC
00843164 ....$15.99

116. JACO PASTORIUS
00843165 ....$15.99

117. ANTONIO CARLOS JOBIM – MORE HITS
00843166 ....$15.99

118. BIG JAZZ STANDARDS COLLECTION
00843167 ....$27.50

119. JELLY ROLL MORTON
00843168 ....$15.99

120. J.S. BACH
00843169 ....$15.99

121. DJANGO REINHARDT
00843170 ....$15.99

122. PAUL SIMON
00843182 ....$16.99

123. BACHARACH & DAVID
00843185 ....$15.99

124. JAZZ-ROCK HORN HITS
00843186 ....$15.99

126. COUNT BASIE CLASSICS
00843157 ....$15.99

127. CHUCK MANGIONE
00843188 ....$15.99

132. STAN GETZ ESSENTIALS
00843193 ....$15.99

133. STAN GETZ FAVORITES
00843194 ....$15.99

134. NURSERY RHYMES*
00843196 ....$17.99

135. JEFF BECK
00843197 ....$15.99

136. NAT ADDERLEY
00843198 ....$15.99

137. WES MONTGOMERY
00843199 ....$15.99

138. FREDDIE HUBBARD
00843200 ....$15.99

139. JULIAN "CANNONBALL" ADDERLEY
00843201 ....$15.99

141. BILL EVANS STANDARDS
00843156 ....$15.99

150. JAZZ IMPROV BASICS
00843195 ....$19.99

151. MODERN JAZZ QUARTET CLASSICS
00843209 ....$15.99

157. HYMNS
00843217 ....$15.99

162. BIG CHRISTMAS COLLECTION
00843221 ....$24.99

*These CDs do not include split tracks.

Jazz Instruction & Improvisation
Books for All Instruments from Hal Leonard

AN APPROACH TO JAZZ IMPROVISATION
by Dave Pozzi
Musicians Institute Press
Explore the styles of Charlie Parker, Sonny Rollins, Bud Powell and others with this comprehensive guide to jazz improvisation. Covers: scale choices • chord analysis • phrasing • melodies • harmonic progressions • more.
00695135 Book/CD Pack $17.95

INCLUDES TAB

BUILDING A JAZZ VOCABULARY
By Mike Steinel
A valuable resource for learning the basics of jazz from Mike Steinel of the University of North Texas. It covers: the basics of jazz • how to build effective solos • a comprehensive practice routine • and a jazz vocabulary of the masters.
00849911 ....$19.95

THE CYCLE OF FIFTHS
by Emile and Laura De Cosmo
This essential instruction book provides more than 450 exercises, including hundreds of melodic and rhythmic ideas. The book is designed to help improvisors master the cycle of fifths, one of the primary progressions in music. Guaranteed to refine technique, enhance improvisational fluency, and improve sight-reading!
00311114 ....$16.99

THE DIATONIC CYCLE
by Emile and Laura De Cosmo
Renowned jazz educators Emile and Laura De Cosmo provide more than 300 exercises to help improvisors tackle one of music's most common progressions: the diatonic cycle. This book is guaranteed to refine technique, enhance improvisational fluency, and improve sight-reading!
00311115 ....$16.95

EAR TRAINING
by Keith Wyatt, Carl Schroeder and Joe Elliott
Musicians Institute Press
Covers: basic pitch matching • singing major and minor scales • identifying intervals • transcribing melodies and rhythm • identifying chords and progressions • seventh chords and the blues • modal interchange, chromaticism, modulation • and more.
00695198 Book/2-CD Pack......................$24.95

EXERCISES AND ETUDES FOR THE JAZZ INSTRUMENTALIST
by J.J. Johnson
Designed as study material and playable by any instrument, these pieces run the gamut of the jazz experience, featuring common and uncommon time signatures and keys, and styles from ballads to funk. They are progressively graded so that both beginners and professionals will be challenged by the demands of this wonderful music.
00842018 Bass Clef Edition....................$16.95
00842042 Treble Clef Edition $16.95

JAZZOLOGY
THE ENCYCLOPEDIA OF JAZZ THEORY FOR ALL MUSICIANS
by Robert Rawlins and Nor Eddine Bahha
This comprehensive resource covers a variety of jazz topics, for beginners and pros of any instrument. The book serves as an encyclopedia for reference, a thorough methodology for the student, and a workbook for the classroom.
00311167 ....$19.99

JAZZ JAM SESSION
15 TRACKS INCLUDING RHYTHM CHANGES, BLUES, BOSSA, BALLADS & MORE
by Ed Friedland
Bring your local jazz jam session home! These essential jazz rhythm grooves feature a professional rhythm section and are perfect for guitar, harmonica, keyboard, saxophone and trumpet players to hone their soloing skills. The feels, tempos and keys have been varied to broaden your jazz experience. Styles include: ballads, bebop, blues, bossa nova, cool jazz, and more, with improv guidelines for each track.
00311827 Book/CD Pack......................$19.99

JAZZ THEORY RESOURCES
by Bert Ligon
Houston Publishing, Inc.
This is a jazz theory text in two volumes. **Volume 1 includes:** review of basic theory • rhythm in jazz performance • triadic generalization • diatonic harmonic progressions and analysis • substitutions and turnarounds • and more. **Volume 2 includes:** modes and modal frameworks • quartal harmony • extended tertian structures and triadic superimposition • pentatonic applications • coloring "outside" the lines and beyond • and more.
00030458 Volume 1 ....$39.95
00030459 Volume 2 ....$29.95

Prices, contents & availability subject to change without notice.

JOY OF IMPROV
by Dave Frank and John Amaral
This book/CD course on improvisation for all instruments and all styles will help players develop monster musical skills! **Book One** imparts a solid basis in technique, rhythm, chord theory, ear training and improv concepts. **Book Two** explores more advanced chord voicings, chord arranging techniques and more challenging blues and melodic lines. The CD can be used as a listening and play-along tool.
00220005 Book 1 – Book/CD Pack $27.99
00220006 Book 2 – Book/CD Pack $24.95

THE PATH TO JAZZ IMPROVISATION
by Emile and Laura De Cosmo
This fascinating jazz instruction book offers an innovative, scholarly approach to the art of improvisation. It includes in-depth analysis and lessons about: cycle of fifths • diatonic cycle • overtone series • pentatonic scale • harmonic and melodic minor scale • polytonal order of keys • blues and bebop scales • modes • and more.
00310904 ....$14.95

THE SOURCE
THE DICTIONARY OF CONTEMPORARY AND TRADITIONAL SCALES
by Steve Barta
This book serves as an informative guide for people who are looking for good, solid information regarding scales, chords, and how they work together. It provides right and left hand fingerings for scales, chords, and complete inversions. Includes over 20 different scales, each written in all 12 keys.
00240885 ....$17.99

21 BEBOP EXERCISES
by Steve Rawlins
This book/CD pack is both a warm-up collection and a manual for bebop phrasing. Its tasty and sophisticated exercises will help you develop your proficiency with jazz interpretation. It concentrates on practice in all twelve keys — moving higher by half-step — to help develop dexterity and range. The companion CD includes all of the exercises in 12 keys.
00315341 Book/CD Pack......................$17.95

0911

ARTIST TRANSCRIPTIONS

Artist Transcriptions are authentic, note-for-note transcriptions of today's hottest artists in jazz, pop and rock. These outstanding, accurate arrangements are in an easy-to-read format which includes all essential lines. Artist Transcriptions can be used to perform, sequence or for reference.

CLARINET

00672423	Buddy De Franco Collection	$19.95

FLUTE

00672379	Eric Dolphy Collection	$19.95
00672372	James Moody Collection – Sax and Flute	$19.95
00660108	James Newton – Improvising Flute	$14.95

GUITAR & BASS

00660113	The Guitar Style of George Benson	$14.95
00699072	Guitar Book of Pierre Bensusan	$29.95
00672331	Ron Carter – Acoustic Bass	$16.95
00672307	Stanley Clarke Collection	$19.95
00660115	Al Di Meola – Friday Night in San Francisco	$14.95
00604043	Al Di Meola – Music, Words, Pictures	$14.95
00673245	Jazz Style of Tal Farlow	$19.95
00672359	Bela Fleck and the Flecktones	$18.95
00699389	Jim Hall – Jazz Guitar Environments	$19.95
00699306	Jim Hall – Exploring Jazz Guitar	$19.95
00604049	Allan Holdsworth – Reaching for the Uncommon Chord	$14.95
00699215	Leo Kottke – Eight Songs	$14.95
00675536	Wes Montgomery – Guitar Transcriptions	$17.95
00672353	Joe Pass Collection	$18.95
00673216	John Patitucci	$16.95
00027083	Django Reinhardt Antholog	$14.95
00026711	Genius of Django Reinhardt	$10.95
00672374	Johnny Smith Guitar Solos	$16.95
00672320	Mark Whitfield	$19.95

PIANO & KEYBOARD

00672338	Monty Alexander Collection	$19.95
00672487	Monty Alexander Plays Standards	$19.95
00672318	Kenny Barron Collection	$22.95
00672520	Count Basie Collection	$19.95
00672364	Warren Bernhardt Collection	$19.95
00672439	Cyrus Chestnut Collection	$19.95
00673242	Billy Childs Collection	$19.95
00672300	Chick Corea – Paint the World	$12.95
00672537	Bill Evans at Town Hall	$16.95
00672425	Bill Evans – Piano Interpretations	$19.95
00672365	Bill Evans – Piano Standards	$19.95
00672510	Bill Evans Trio – Vol. 1: 1959-1961	$24.95
00672511	Bill Evans Trio – Vol. 2: 1962-1965	$24.95
00672512	Bill Evans Trio – Vol. 3: 1968-1974	$24.95
00672513	Bill Evans Trio – Vol. 4: 1979-1980	$24.95
00672381	Tommy Flanagan Collection	$24.99
00672492	Benny Goodman Collection	$16.95
00672486	Vince Guaraldi Collection	$19.95
00672419	Herbie Hancock Collection	$19.95
00672438	Hampton Hawes	$19.95

00672322	Ahmad Jamal Collection	$22.95
00672564	Best of Jeff Lorber	$17.99
00672476	Brad Mehldau Collection	$19.99
00672388	Best of Thelonious Monk	$19.95
00672389	Thelonious Monk Collection	$19.95
00672390	Thelonious Monk Plays Jazz Standards – Volume 1	$19.95
00672391	Thelonious Monk Plays Jazz Standards – Volume 2	$19.95
00672433	Jelly Roll Morton – The Piano Rolls	$12.95
00672553	Charlie Parker for Piano	$19.95
00672542	Oscar Peterson – Jazz Piano Solos	$16.95
00672544	Oscar Peterson – Originals	$9.95
00672532	Oscar Peterson – Plays Broadway	$19.95
00672531	Oscar Peterson – Plays Duke Ellington	$19.95
00672563	Oscar Peterson – A Royal Wedding Suite	$19.99
00672533	Oscar Peterson – Trios	$24.95
00672543	Oscar Peterson Trio – Canadiana Suite	$9.95
00672534	Very Best of Oscar Peterson	$22.95
00672371	Bud Powell Classics	$19.95
00672376	Bud Powell Collection	$19.95
00672437	André Previn Collection	$19.95
00672507	Gonzalo Rubalcaba Collection	$19.95
00672303	Horace Silver Collection	$19.95
00672316	Art Tatum Collection	$22.95
00672355	Art Tatum Solo Book	$19.95
00672357	Billy Taylor Collection	$24.95
00673215	McCoy Tyner	$16.95
00672321	Cedar Walton Collection	$19.95
00672519	Kenny Werner Collection	$19.95
00672434	Teddy Wilson Collection	$19.95

SAXOPHONE

00672566	The Mindi Abair Collection	$14.99
00673244	Julian "Cannonball" Adderley Collection	$19.95
00673237	Michael Brecker	$19.95
00672429	Michael Brecker Collection	$19.95
00672315	Benny Carter Plays Standards	$22.95
00672314	Benny Carter Collection	$22.95
00672394	James Carter Collection	$19.95
00672349	John Coltrane Plays Giant Steps	$19.95
00672529	John Coltrane – Giant Steps	$14.95
00672494	John Coltrane – A Love Supreme	$14.95
00672493	John Coltrane Plays "Coltrane Changes"	$19.95
00672453	John Coltrane Plays Standards	$19.95
00673233	John Coltrane Solos	$22.95
00672328	Paul Desmond Collection	$19.95
00672379	Eric Dolphy Collection	$19.95
00672530	Kenny Garrett Collection	$19.95
00699375	Stan Getz	$19.95
00672377	Stan Getz – Bossa Novas	$19.95
00672375	Stan Getz – Standards	$18.95
00673254	Great Tenor Sax Solos	$18.95

00672523	Coleman Hawkins Collection	$19.95
00673252	Joe Henderson – Selections from "Lush Life" & "So Near So Far"	$19.95
00672330	Best of Joe Henderson	$22.95
00673239	Best of Kenny G	$19.95
00673229	Kenny G – Breathless	$19.95
00672462	Kenny G – Classics in the Key of G	$19.95
00672485	Kenny G – Faith: A Holiday Album	$14.95
00672373	Kenny G – The Moment	$19.95
00672326	Joe Lovano Collection	$19.95
00672498	Jackie McLean Collection	$19.95
00672372	James Moody Collection – Sax and Flute	$19.95
00672416	Frank Morgan Collection	$19.95
00672539	Gerry Mulligan Collection	$19.95
00672352	Charlie Parker Collection	$19.95
00672561	Best of Sonny Rollins	$19.95
00672444	Sonny Rollins Collection	$19.95
00675000	David Sanborn Collection	$17.95
00672528	Bud Shank Collection	$19.95
00672491	New Best of Wayne Shorter	$19.95
00672550	The Sonny Stitt Collection	$19.95
00672350	Tenor Saxophone Standards	$18.95
00672567	The Best of Kim Waters	$17.99
00672524	Lester Young Collection	$19.95

TROMBONE

00672332	J.J. Johnson Collection	$19.95
00672489	Steve Turré Collection	$19.95

TRUMPET

00672557	Herb Alpert Collection	$14.99
00672480	Louis Armstrong Collection	$17.95
00672481	Louis Armstrong Plays Standards	$17.95
00672435	Chet Baker Collection	$19.95
00672556	Best of Chris Botti	$19.95
00672448	Miles Davis – Originals, Vol. 1	$19.95
00672451	Miles Davis – Originals, Vol. 2	$19.95
00672450	Miles Davis – Standards, Vol. 1	$19.95
00672449	Miles Davis – Standards, Vol. 2	$19.95
00672479	Dizzy Gillespie Collection	$19.95
00673214	Freddie Hubbard	$14.95
00672382	Tom Harrell – Jazz Trumpet	$19.95
00672363	Jazz Trumpet Solos	$9.95
00672506	Chuck Mangione Collection	$19.95
00672525	Arturo Sandoval – Trumpet Evolution	$19.95

FOR MORE INFORMATION, SEE YOUR LOCAL MUSIC DEALER, OR WRITE TO:

HAL•LEONARD® CORPORATION

7777 W. BLUEMOUND RD. P.O. BOX 13819 MILWAUKEE, WI 53213

Visit our web site for a complete listing of our titles with songlists at
www.halleonard.com

0310

The Best-Selling Jazz Book of All Time Is Now Legal!

The Real Books are the most popular jazz books of all time. Since the 1970s, musicians have trusted these volumes to get them through every gig, night after night. The problem is that the books were illegally produced and distributed, without any regard to copyright law, or royalties paid to the composers who created these musical masterpieces.

Hal Leonard is very proud to present the first legitimate and legal editions of these books ever produced. You won't even notice the difference, other than all the notorious errors being fixed: the covers and typeface look the same, the song lists are nearly identical, and the price for our edition is even cheaper than the originals!

Every conscientious musician will appreciate that these books are now produced accurately and ethically, benefitting the songwriters that we owe for some of the greatest tunes of all time!

VOLUME 1
Includes: Autumn Leaves • Body and Soul • Don't Get Around Much Anymore • Falling in Love with Love • Have You Met Miss Jones? • Lullaby of Birdland • Misty • Satin Doll • Stella by Starlight • and hundreds more!

00240221	C Edition	$29.99
00240224	B♭ Edition	$29.95
00240225	E♭ Edition	$29.99
00240226	Bass Clef Edition	$29.95
00240292	C Edition 6 x 9	$27.95
00451087	C Edition on CD-ROM	$25.00

VOLUME 2
Includes: Avalon • Birdland • Come Rain or Come Shine • Fever • Georgia on My Mind • It Might as Well Be Spring • Moonglow • The Nearness of You • On the Sunny Side of the Street • Route 66 • Sentimental Journey • Smoke Gets in Your Eyes • Tangerine • Yardbird Suite • and more!

00240222	C Edition	$29.99
00240227	B♭ Edition	$29.95
00240228	E♭ Edition	$29.95
00240229	Bass Clef Edition	$29.95
00240293	C Edition 6 x 9	$27.95

VOLUME 3
Includes: Ain't Misbehavin' • Cheek to Cheek • The Lady Is a Tramp • A Nightingale Sang in Berkeley Square • On a Clear Day • Stormy Weather • The Very Thought of You • and more!

00240233	C Edition	$29.99
00240284	B♭ Edition	$29.95
00240285	E♭ Edition	$29.95
00240286	Bass Clef Edition	$29.95

VOLUME 4
Includes: The Best Is Yet to Come • A Foggy Day (In London Town) • I Got Rhythm • Kansas City • Night and Day • Ol' Man River • Smile • Them There Eyes • and more!

00240296	C Edition	$29.99

Play-along CDs to some of the most popular songs featured in the world famous *Real Books* are available. Each volume features selections sorted alphabetically from the 6th edition, each in 3-CD sets.

The Real Book Play-Along – Volume 1

00240302	A-D	$24.99
00240303	E-J	$24.95
00240304	L-R	$24.95
00240305	S-Z	$24.99

The Real Book Play-Along – Volume 2

00240351	A-D	$24.99
00240352	E-I	$24.99
00240353	J-R	$24.99
00240354	S-Z	$24.99

Also available:

00240264	The Real Blues Book	$34.99
00240306	The Real Christmas Book	$25.00
00240137	Miles Davis Real Book	$19.95
00240235	The Duke Ellington Real Book	$19.99
00240331	The Bud Powell Real Book	$19.99
00240313	The Real Rock Book	$29.99
00240359	The Real Tab Book – Vol. 1	$32.50
00310910	The Real Bluegrass Book	$29.99
00240355	The Real Dixieland Book	$29.99
00240317	The Real Worship Book	$29.99

THE REAL VOCAL BOOK

00240230	Volume 1 High Voice	$29.95
00240307	Volume 1 Low Voice	$29.99
00240231	Volume 2 High Voice	$29.95
00240308	Volume 2 Low Voice	$29.95

THE REAL BOOK – STAFF PAPER

00240327		$9.95

Complete song lists online at www.halleonard.com
Prices and availability subject to change without notice.

0111